Al Qaeda

Osama bin Laden's Army of Terrorists

Phillip Margulies

The Rosen Publishing Group, Inc.
New York

To the victims of the terrorist attacks of September 11, 2001

Published in 2003 by The Rosen Publishing Group, Inc.
29 East 21st Street, New York, NY 10010

Library of Congress Cataloging-in-Publication Data

Margulies, Phillip.
Al Qaeda : Osama bin Laden's army of terrorists / Phillip Margulies.—
1st ed.
    p. cm. — (Inside the world's most infamous terrorist organizations)
Summary: Discusses the Islamic organization known as Al Qaeda, focusing on its presumed role in the September 11 terrorist attacks in the United States.
Includes bibliographical references and index.
ISBN 0-8239-3817-4
1. Terrorism. 2. Qaida (Organization) 3. Jihad. 4. September 11 Terrorist Attacks, 2001. 5. War on Terrorism, 2001– [1. Terrorism. 2. Qaida (Organization) 3. September 11 Terrorist Attacks, 2001.]
I. Title. II. Series.
HV6431 .M3646 2003
973.931—dc21

                                                          2002007526

Manufactured in the United States of America

Contents

Introduction

Terrorism is a spectacle. Unlike most criminals, terrorists want their actions to be witnessed. They want as many people as possible to see, hear, discuss, and read about what they have done. By that grisly standard, the attacks against the United States on September 11, 2001, were a stunning success. Four hijacked airliners, with a total of 246 passengers on board, were turned into bombs and flown into the symbols of American pride, wealth, and power. Two crashed into the World Trade Center towers in New York City. One struck the Pentagon in Arlington, Virginia (a suburb of Washington, D.C.). The fourth, perhaps on a collision course with the White House or the U.S. Capitol, crashed in a Pennsylvania field while its passengers struggled with the hijackers.

As the world watched in horror, the twin towers of the World Trade Center collapsed, killing almost 3,000 trapped workers and rescuers. This nightmarish scene of unimaginable cruelty, suffering, and loss will be seared in our memories forever.

Trying to find a bright spot within these dark events—some evidence of the better side of human nature—reporters dwelled on the courage of the rescuers who rushed into the burning buildings, driven by a sense of duty that overrode their natural instinct

A rescue helicopter surveys the damage to the Pentagon as firefighters battle flames after an airplane hijacked by members of Al Qaeda crashed into the Department of Defense's headquarters in Arlington, Virginia, on September 11, 2001. The deliberate crash of American Airlines Flight 77 into the Pentagon killed 125 Defense Department employees and the 65 passengers and crew members on board the plane.

for self-preservation. These men and women may not have known they were going to die, but they knew that they were putting their lives in jeopardy as they went straight into the burning, smoking nightmare so many others were desperately trying to escape. Courage like theirs is truly awe-inspiring.

With the Brooklyn Bridge in the foreground, United Airlines Flight 175 explodes after hitting the south tower of the World Trade Center at 9:03 AM on September 11, 2001. The north tower *(right)* is already smoking following the crash of American Airlines Flight 11 into its side eighteen minutes earlier. By 10:29 AM, both towers had collapsed. About 2,823 office workers, firefighters, police officers, and rescue workers died in the towers, along with 157 passengers and crew members on the two airplanes.

Sadly, the events of September 11 also revealed a side of human nature that is even harder to understand. Nineteen others—the hijackers—also died, sacrificing their lives to create the horror of that day. Once they got their orders, most of them probably knew they were going to die. Did they doubt that what they were doing was right? Nothing in their actions leading up to the attacks indicates that they did. They wrote farewell letters for their loved ones to read when they were gone. A London newspaper, *The Observer*, quoted a letter dated September 10 from the twenty-six-year-old hijacker Ziad Jarrah to his girlfriend, Ayse Sengun, who lived in Germany, as reading, "I did what I had to do, and you should be very proud of that. It is a great honour, and you will see the result, and everyone will be celebrating." The hijackers commended their souls to God as they prepared to kill thousands of innocent men, women, and children.

These men all belonged to a group known as Al Qaeda (Arabic for "the foundation" or "the base"), which had proven itself, even before September 11, to be among the most dangerous terrorist organizations in the world. Its ultimate aim, according to the U.S. government, is to unite all Muslims and establish a government that follows the rule of the Caliphs (the spiritual heads of Islam, viewed as direct successors of the prophet Muhammad, the founder of Islam). That is, Al Qaeda's members believe that all Muslim countries should have a single ruler, and the Koran should be the law of the land. For this to happen, the secular (non-religious) governments of most countries in which Muslims are the majority would have to fall. So Al Qaeda threatens most of the existing governments of the Middle East, as well as some in Africa and Asia.

Introduction

The United States, because of its influence in the region, is the primary target of Al Qaeda's wrath. To Al Qaeda, and to many others who share the beliefs of its members, the United States is "the Great Satan." They hate the United States for its secular lifestyle, which Muslim clerics feel lures followers away from Islam; for the presence of American soldiers in Muslim lands; and for the United States's support of Israel, the Jewish homeland that has long been in conflict with its Arab neighbors and occupies land that most Muslims believe belongs to the Palestinians. In February 1998, Al Qaeda's leader, Osama bin Laden, added his name to a *fatwa*—an Islamic religious ruling—about the United States. According to the Federal Bureau of Investigation (FBI), bin Laden and other religious leaders who issued the fatwa stated that "to kill the Americans and their allies, including civilians and military, is an individual duty for every Muslim who can do it in any country in which it is possible to do it."

This dire pronouncement, largely ignored by the American public when it was issued, would bear poisonous fruit three and a half years later, on September 11, 2001.

Mujahedeen

W e have come to call it Al Qaeda, but over the years the terrorist organization behind the September 11 attacks has had several other names. It is also known as the Islamic Army for the Liberation of the Holy Places, the World Islamic Front for Jihad Against Jews and Crusaders, and the Islamic Salvation Foundation. Sometimes it is simply referred to as "the Osama bin Laden terror network."

Jihad and the Cold War

Al Qaeda's beginnings date from the last decade of the Cold War between the United States and the Soviet Union, a period of pro- longed hostility between the superpowers marked not by open war- fare but by an arms race and attempts to influence the governments of other countries. The Soviets had invaded Afghanistan in 1979 to prop up a secular pro-Communist government friendly to Soviet interests. Thousands of volunteers from around the Middle East came to fight beside their fellow Muslims against the "godless" Marxist regime. These were the mujahedeen—Muslim holy war- riors. Many came from Saudi Arabia and were members of the Wahhabi, a fundamentalist Islamic sect to which the royal family of Saudi Arabia belongs. For these young men, the war in Afghanistan was an opportunity to prove their bravery and commitment to Islam. It was a jihad, or holy war, in defense of the Islamic faith.

Soviet tanks line up along a street in Kabul, the capital city of Afghanistan, in 1981. The Soviet invasion of Afghanistan lasted for nine years and ultimately ended in the Red Army's retreat. Despite the Soviets' strong military advantage, they were unable to defeat the Afghan guerrillas, who were backed by both Osama bin Laden and the United States.

Throughout much of the 1980s, the mujahedeen and the United States were allies in Afghanistan. The United States supplied the Afghan fighters with money and weapons. So did the "Arabi," as the Afghan nationals called the Arab volunteers. The alliance was temporary because in the long run the United States and the mujahedeen wanted very different things. The United

States wanted to drive the Soviet Union out of Afghanistan in order to counter its influence in the region. For the mujahedeen, expelling the Soviets was only the first step in an Islamic revolution that they hoped would sweep the entire Middle East.

The aims of the United States and the mujahedeen in Afghanistan were bound to collide one day. But there is an old saying that goes "the enemy of my enemy is my friend." For the time being, what counted to the United States was that the mujahedeen were the enemies of the Soviet Union.

Osama bin Laden

Osama bin Laden was a member of a rich Saudi Arabian family. He was one of the first of the mujahedeen to come to Afghanistan to resist Soviet occupation. In the mid-1980s, he began providing money to a group that recruited Muslims from around the world to fight in Afghanistan. These Muslims, who traveled to central Asia from the Arab countries, were very well funded. With their new weapons, new vehicles, and new clothing, they formed a stark contrast to the impoverished Afghans, who were often poorly clothed, freezing, and starving. Western relief workers and journalists called these Arab fighters "the Gucci mujahedeen" (after the expensive designer brand Gucci).

In Afghanistan, a place that has endured many years of brutal warfare and is no stranger to extreme violence, the Arabi nevertheless earned a reputation for ruthlessness. They were best known for their tendency to kill those they captured, completely ignoring international conventions on the treatment of prisoners of war and innocent civilians. The Arabi were also involved in violence directed at journalists and relief workers. It is ordinarily understood that they are neutral parties to any conflict and not to be mistreated. This violence included beatings, kidnappings, and attacks on vehicles.

The Arabi didn't just want to push the Soviets out of Afghanistan in order to liberate their non-Arab Muslim brothers and sisters. They wanted to decide who ruled Afghanistan later, even though this was not their country. For them, the desire to create a unified Islamic state overrode any concern for national boundaries. To help achieve this aim, rich Arabi like Osama bin Laden paid money to Afghan guerrilla commanders to buy their loyalty.

The Rise of the Taliban

Finally, in 1988, the Soviet withdrawal from the country began. The Afghan people, however, did not enjoy a richly deserved period of peace, as factions within Afghanistan quickly turned to warring against each other. The winners of this prolonged struggle turned out to be an extreme fundamentalist group, the Taliban (which means "seekers of truth" in Arabic), who took control of the capital city of Kabul in 1996 and ruled most of the country by 1998.

The victory over the Soviets in Afghanistan boosted the morale of Islamic fundamentalists. They had taken on a superpower and won. More important, they had installed a regime that, in the name of restoring order to a country plagued by banditry and civil war following the Soviet withdrawal, imposed a very harsh, conservative interpretation of Islamic law on all Afghans.

These Afghan women dressed in burqas are begging for help in Kandahar, Afghanistan. A burqa is a long garment with only a grid at eye level through which to see. Burqas are worn by many Muslim women to drape their bodies. These women may remove their burqas only when in the presence of close relatives and female friends. In public, the burqa must always be worn. Although the Koran does not require women to be covered completely in public, many conservative Islamic countries demand that women be veiled.

Many Afghans were grateful at first for this firm hand. The Taliban proceeded, however, to strictly curtail basic freedoms in its desire to create a perfect Islamic state. Televisions, non-religious music, dancing, movies, photography, paintings, statues, and even kite flying and cheering at soccer games were suddenly banned.

Some of the most severe restrictions were placed upon women, who were no longer allowed to work or attend school. Outside their homes, Afghan women had to wear a burqa, a garment that covers every part of the body except the eyes. Religious police patrolled the country in pickup trucks, carrying sticks with which they would beat anyone caught violating the rules. The Taliban made hand amputations the punishment for theft, and death by stoning the punishment for adultery.

After the Soviet withdrawal from Afghanistan, Osama bin Laden returned to Saudi Arabia, where he started an organization to help veterans of the Afghan War. Many of these former mujahedeen went on to fight in other wars that involved Muslim combatants, including conflicts in Somalia and Bosnia. These traveling warriors would form the core of Al Qaeda.

Obviously, these Muslim extremists were no friends of the United States, even in the 1980s when they were joined in an alliance of convenience. Two events in particular fueled the anger of many Islamic fundamentalists against the United States: the Gulf War and Operation Restore Hope in Somalia, two U.S.-led "incursions" into Muslim lands.

The Gulf War

In 1990, the Iraqi army of Saddam Hussein invaded its tiny, oil-rich Persian Gulf neighbor, Kuwait. The move was threatening to other Gulf nations, who felt that Hussein might try to invade them next. It was also opposed by Islamic fundamentalists, since Iraq is a secular state. Osama bin Laden asked the Saudi royal family to let him and his mujahedeen expel the Iraqis from Kuwait, as they had helped expel the Soviets from Afghanistan. Perhaps fearing the extremism of bin Laden and his followers, the Saudis instead sought help from the United States, which was itself concerned that any disruption in oil production and supply as a result of the Iraqi invasion would lead to higher oil and gas prices and harm the U.S. economy.

To drive Iraq out of Kuwait, the United States moved hundreds of thousands of U.S. soldiers to Saudi Arabia and established military bases there. To prevent another invasion by the still powerful though defeated Hussein, the bases remained after the Gulf War was over and Kuwait's freedom had been regained. This U.S. presence was an outrage to Islamic extremist groups. Saudi Arabia is the birthplace of Islam. Mecca and Medina, the two holiest cities of the Muslim religion, are located in Saudi Arabia. The Koran, the Muslims' holy book, bans non-Muslims from the Arabian Peninsula. Islamic fundamentalists regard the presence of infidel, or unbelieving, U.S. soldiers as a defilement of their holy places.

Operation Restore Hope

A second grievance against the United States among Islamic fundamentalists like bin Laden and his Al Qaeda mujahedeen arose from a United Nations peacekeeping mission, not a territorial war. In the

Iraqi troops emerge from a heavily protected bunker in southeast Kuwait to surrender to Saudi soldiers during Operation Desert Storm in February 1991. Saudi participation in the U.S.-led attempt to turn back the Iraqi invasion of Kuwait enraged Osama bin Laden, as did the presence of American soldiers in Saudi Arabia. Both of these "outrages" are thought to have fueled his desire to launch terrorist attacks against the United States.

early 1990s, Somalia, a country with a large Muslim population in an area known as the Horn of Africa, was in the grip of a civil war. Somalia's central government had lost control of the country. The people of Somalia were starving because the war was preventing humanitarian groups from distributing food.

In December 1992, a U.N. force led by around 2,000 United States Marines was sent to restore order. It was the first time the United Nations had ever intervened in the affairs of an independent state without the permission and invitation of that country's government.

Operation Restore Hope was a very different mission than the Gulf War. It was conducted on a much smaller scale, had primarily humanitarian aims, and in many ways was a failure. U.N. forces were unable to stop the bloodshed. By the time the operation was called off, about 50,000 people had been killed in fighting between warlords. Around 300,000 Somalians died of starvation because the fighting made transportation of relief supplies impossible. The United States became embroiled in a manhunt for a Somali warlord, General Mohammad Farrah Aidid, but did not succeed in finding him. U.S. soldiers were trapped in ambushes, and people back home were horrified to see videos of the dead bodies of American soldiers dragged through the streets of Mogadishu (Somalia's capital city) by angry mobs.

Although the United States went to Somalia to help feed starving people and prevent further killing, some Islamic fundamentalists saw peacekeeping as an excuse for American occupation of Muslim lands. In addition, the United States made enemies among the people it was trying to save when civilians were killed in a failed attempt to capture General Aidid.

In 1992 and 1993, bin Laden and other Al Qaeda members pronounced fatwas stating that the American forces stationed in the Horn of Africa, including Somalia, should be attacked. Al Qaeda members ordered military training for Somali tribes opposed to the

Major Strikes Attributed to Al Qaeda

- The killing of U.S. soldiers in Somalia
- The 1993 bombing of the World Trade Center
- The 1996 bombing of U.S. barracks in Saudi Arabia
- The 1998 bombing of U.S. Embassies in East Africa, which killed 224 people (mostly East African civilians) and wounded many others
- A foiled 1999 plot to bomb the millennium celebrations in Seattle, Washington
- The bombing in 2000 of the USS *Cole* in a port in Yemen, killing 17 U.S. sailors
- The attacks of September 11, 2001

United Nations intervention there. Bin Laden later claimed that men trained by him helped kill 128 American servicemen in the Horn of Africa, including eighteen in Somalia. These attacks are the first known actions by Al Qaeda against U.S. citizens.

America's horror at the deaths of the marines in Mogadishu—a strong public reaction that led to an early end to America's involvement in the mission—made a profound impression on Al Qaeda. In later interviews, according to reports in *Time* magazine, bin Laden said he and the other Al Qaeda members had expected the American soldiers and public to be tough like the Soviets. Instead, they had turned out to be "paper tigers," because "after a few blows [they] ran in defeat."

Inside Al Qaeda

Osama bin Laden, whose whereabouts at the time of this writing are unknown, is the backbone of Al Qaeda—its organizer, financial backer, and spiritual guide. But beyond that, who is he? Osama bin Laden is one of fifty-two children fathered by Mohammed bin Laden (who, like many wealthy Muslims, had several wives). Through close ties to the royal family of Saudi Arabia, Mohammed bin Laden built a construction business into a multibillion-dollar empire. Today, the business, called the bin Laden Group, employs 37,000 people worldwide. It has no connection to terrorist activity, and most of the family have disavowed Osama's actions.

Osama bin Laden is a product of this very comfortable life. His anger and violence, however, seem to have very different sources.

From Privilege to Jihad

Osama bin Laden spent a comfortable childhood amid air-conditioned houses, private horse stables, and servants. At the age of thirteen, when his father died, he inherited $80 million. As a young man, he was a pious Muslim. He married his first wife when he was only seventeen years old and attended college at the King Abdul Aziz University in Jedda, where he studied civil engineering. He graduated with a degree in economics and public

This is a video image taken by Al-Jazeera (a news agency often referred to as the Arabic CNN) of Osama bin Laden riding a horse in Afghanistan in 1998. After being expelled from Sudan under pressure from the U.S. government, bin Laden moved the headquarters of his Al Qaeda terrorist operation to Afghanistan, where the ultraconservative Islamic fundamentalist ruling party, the Taliban, welcomed him and offered him promises of protection.

administration. By all appearances, Osama bin Laden was a peaceful, productive member of Saudi Arabian society. What happened to transform him into one of history's most notorious and violent terrorists? When asked later what started him on the path to jihad, bin Laden mentioned three key events, according to the *New York Times*.

The first spark to bin Laden's fury was the 1978 peace treaty between Egypt and Israel, which was negotiated and encouraged by U.S. president Jimmy Carter at Camp David (a presidential retreat outside Washington, D.C.). Egyptian president Anwar Sadat became the first Arab leader to declare that Israel had a right to exist. He, along with Israeli prime minister Menachem Begin, was awarded the 1978 Nobel Peace Prize for his efforts. Sadat was assassinated in 1981 by Egyptian Islamic extremists for what they considered an unacceptable compromise with Israel and a betrayal of Islamic interests.

The second inspiration to jihad for bin Laden was the 1979 Iranian revolution in which the Western-supported leader, the Shah, was dethroned and sent into exile. Though the Shah's overthrow was backed by many groups in Iran—including nonreligious Marxists and people who simply wanted a less corrupt and dictatorial government—Islamic fundamentalists soon gained the upper hand. Their strict interpretation of the Koran became the law of the land. A religious leader and guiding spirit of the revolution, the Ayatollah Khomeini, became the most powerful man in Iran. Like many Islamic fundamentalists around the world, Osama bin Laden was inspired by Khomeini's example of how to defeat Western interests and install a strong and enduring Islamic regime.

The third event that Osama bin Laden mentioned as a motivation for his terrorist jihad was the 1979 Soviet invasion of Afghanistan. According to Koranic law, no land that has been inhabited by Muslims can ever be permitted to fall into infidel hands. So, for Islamic fundamentalists like bin Laden, the Soviets had offended God, and the struggle against their armed occupation became a holy war.

Dreams of the Caliphate
and the Birth of Al Qaeda

While these events probably did help bring about Osama bin Laden's entry into religious politics, he was also influenced by a teacher. At King Abdul Aziz University, Osama bin Laden met Sheikh Abdullah Azzam. A Palestinian, Azzam was a leader of the Muslim Brotherhood, a group that favored a Muslim religious revival. Azzam also inspired Osama bin Laden to dream of bringing back the Caliphate—the Islamic government that had once united all Muslims under a single ruler. In Azzam's vision, even Spain, where Muslims have not ruled since the fifteenth century, would once again be a Muslim country ruled by the Koran. Together, Azzam and bin Laden cofounded the Maktab al-Khidamat (MAK), or Services Office, a group created to help raise and funnel money to the Afghan resistance. Many of the members of this group later joined Al Qaeda.

In 1991, bin Laden moved to Sudan, where Islamic fundamentalists had recently taken power. Using Sudan as a base of operations and raising money through a legitimate construction business, he built up the resources of Al Qaeda, recruiting members and stockpiling weapons. In addition to his secret activities in forming this new terrorist group, he publicly advocated the overthrow of the Saudi government. Alarmed by this, Saudi Arabia revoked Osama bin Laden's citizenship in 1994, and his family disowned him.

In 1996, under pressure from the United States, the Sudanese government expelled bin Laden. Looking back now, it seems that this may have been a mistake. Bin Laden and his core organization simply moved to Afghanistan, then ruled by the world's most extreme Islamic fundamentalist regime. Under the Taliban, Afghanistan had become an outlaw nation, officially recognized by very few other nations. It was harder to keep watch over Al Qaeda's activities in Afghanistan than it had been in Sudan, and the Taliban and Al Qaeda quickly formed an alliance that would unleash extreme violence both within Afghanistan and beyond.

The Al Qaeda Leadership

One of bin Laden's right-hand men was Dr. Ayman al-Zawahiri, a member of a rich Egyptian family and a founder of the terrorist group Al-Jihad (also known as Egyptian Islamic Jihad). Al-Zawahiri was tortured in prison for Al-Jihad's involvement in the assassination of Anwar Sadat. In Afghanistan, he became Osama bin Laden's personal physician. His daughter married bin Laden's eldest son, Mohammed. Al-Zawahiri is suspected of helping organize the 1997 massacre of sixty-seven foreign tourists at Luxor, the popular Egyptian site that includes the temples and tombs of the Valley of Kings. For these and other actions, he was tried in absentia (without being present) and sentenced to death by an Egyptian court. He has never returned to Egypt to face the charges or receive punishment, and his present whereabouts are unknown.

Another important Al Qaeda military leader was Muhammad Atef. One of the veterans of the Afghan War, Atef was introduced to Osama bin Laden by Dr. al-Zawahiri. He is suspected of planning the 1998 bombings of two U.S. Embassies in the East African countries of Kenya and Tanzania, as well as the September 11, 2001, attacks on the Pentagon and World Trade Center. Atef was killed in a U.S. bombing raid outside Kabul, Afghanistan, in November 2001.

Osama bin Laden in the Islamic World

Many Islamic political leaders around the world have branded Osama bin Laden a criminal. Islamic law, they say, can never be used to justify murder. After the September 11 attacks, even the Ayatollah Ali Khamenei of Iran, a strict Islamic fundamentalist leader, called the fight against terrorism a "holy war."

Not all of the people in Muslim countries agree with their leaders, however. Many revere Osama bin Laden as a sort of folk hero who humbled the powerful forces of the West and waged war on behalf of millions of poor and uneducated Muslims. After September 11, some Muslims interviewed by Western journalists praised Osama bin Laden and rejoiced over the attacks. Others refused to believe that he could be responsible for committing such an atrocity. In many Muslim nations, newspapers reported that the attacks in New York and Washington were somehow committed by Jews in order to cause a war between the United States and Islam.

The Organization's Inner Workings

The links that connected Muhammad Atef, Dr. Ayman al-Zawahiri, and Osama bin Laden were not merely between individuals involved in similar terrorist activities. Instead, the three men formed a close cooperation between two terrorist groups, Al Qaeda and Al-Jihad. Al-Jihad was responsible for the assassination of Anwar Sadat, as well as the attempted assassinations of other Egyptian leaders—President Hosni Mubarak (1995), Interior Minister Hassan al-Alfi (1993), and Prime Minister Atef Sedky (1993). Other Al-Jihad attacks include the unsuccessful plot to

A gunman from the Al-Jihad terrorist group, wearing an Egyptian army uniform, fires an automatic rifle into a parade-reviewing stand during an attack that killed Egyptian president Anwar Sadat in a Cairo suburb on October 6, 1981. Sadat had been watching a military parade commemorating the Arab-Israeli war of October 1973. *Inset:* A *Time* magazine cover from 1978 proclaims Sadat "Man of the Year" for his role in forging a peace agreement with Israel. Many Islamic extremists saw this treaty as a betrayal of Arab interests, and it was the reason Al-Jihad decided to assassinate Sadat.

bomb U.S. and Israeli Embassies in Manila, the Philippines (1994), the bombing of the Egyptian Embassy in Islamabad, Pakistan (1995), and an unsuccessful plot to bomb the U.S. Embassy in Albania (1998). Al Qaeda has many alliances similar to this with other like-minded terrorist groups around the world, in many cases offering them training and funding.

Until recently, most of what was known about Al Qaeda's inner workings came from witnesses who had turned state's evidence (agreed to testify against one's accomplices in return for less jail time or immunity from prosecution) in criminal trials and from the investigative work of police and intelligence (spy) organizations. More has been learned recently from paper documents and computer disks left behind by members of Al Qaeda and the Taliban fleeing U.S. air strikes in Afghanistan.

In memos on computer disks found in Kabul, Afghanistan, Al Qaeda members call their organization "the company" and its leaders "the general management." This led the *Wall Street Journal* to suggest that Al Qaeda is "run like a multinational corporation." A book by a CNN reporter, Peter L. Bergen, called Al Qaeda "Holy War, Inc." Al Qaeda's largest attacks must have called for the kind of central planning, budgeting, research, coordination, communications, and personnel management more often associated with sophisticated and wealthy Western companies than with ragtag, low-tech terrorist groups.

Other observers of Al Qaeda point out, however, that the day-to-day details of terrorist activities are probably not managed from the top. Ahmed Ressam, an Algerian terrorist who cooperated with police after being arrested in December 1999, has said that Al Qaeda agents are seldom given detailed instructions. Instead, they are trained and then sent out to act on their own, as they see fit and as opportunities present themselves. Away from their home base, Al Qaeda members are organized into small groups called cells. Each agent is given only the information he needs to successfully perform his task within the planned terrorist strike. This division of tasks helps ensure that captured Al Qaeda members cannot reveal details of other upcoming attacks when being interrogated by the authorities. It has been estimated that Al Qaeda has cells in over fifty countries. As many as 11,000 men are said to have been trained in Al Qaeda camps in Afghanistan before the downfall of the Taliban led to the abandonment of these camps.

To prevent detection by police profilers (detectives who try to identify terrorists based upon certain typical criteria, such as appearance, behavior, living situation, travel patterns, and financial transactions), Al Qaeda's agents do whatever is necessary to blend in with the population of the country in which they are living. Their instruction booklets tell them to shave their beards, uncover their heads, wear cologne, and carry cigarettes so that they do not fit the typical profile of a religiously observant and fundamentalist Muslim. Al Qaeda operatives in the United States are thought to hold regular jobs while awaiting orders. Others travel around the country or back and forth to Europe carrying money to buy weapons and the everyday objects that can be turned into weapons: pickup trucks, flight instructions, box cutters, and airline tickets.

High Tech and Low Tech

While planning their terrorist operations throughout the 1990s, Al Qaeda used modern communications equipment, including e-mail, faxes, and cell phones. The United States's National Security

U.S. Attorney General John Ashcroft shows off an Al Qaeda training manual during testimony before the Senate Judiciary Committee on December 6, 2001. Ashcroft wants captured and suspected Al Qaeda operatives tried before military tribunals rather than in public criminal trials. In a military tribunal, the accused has limited access to lawyers, is not presumed innocent until proven guilty, does not have to be found guilty "beyond a reasonable doubt," and has no right to appeal a guilty verdict. Many human rights advocates have criticized the U.S. government's decision to use these tribunals to try suspected terrorists.

Agency (NSA) took advantage of this fact to listen in on bin Laden's laptop satellite telephone conversations. Beginning in November 1996, the NSA recorded or traced hundreds of calls on bin Laden's phone to or from England, Yemen, Sudan, Iran, Saudi Arabia, Pakistan, Azerbaijan, and Kenya.

It became harder for the NSA to listen in on bin Laden after the 1998 Al Qaeda attack on the U.S. Embassies in Kenya and Tanzania, however. In retaliation for these bombings, the United States tried to kill bin Laden with cruise missiles. His supposed location was determined using surveillance information provided by the NSA and gathered from intercepted electronic communications. The attack missed its intended target, enabling bin Laden to regroup and continue plotting further terrorist actions. The failed missile attack had an unintended consequence for the United States, however: It made bin Laden realize that high-tech Internet and satellite communications could reveal his location. So he changed his methods. He began to communicate mostly by couriers, who hand-delivered coded instructions and guidance to operatives in Pakistan, who in turn contacted the appropriate agents with their orders. Top Al Qaeda members also sent e-mails that used sophisticated encryption software to frustrate NSA code breakers.

Since at least 1996, the United States considered Osama bin Laden a serious menace and knew that he was planning large-scale attacks on the United States. The administration of President Bill Clinton tried repeatedly to capture or kill him. The new difficulty in intercepting, tracing, and decoding Al Qaeda's communications, however, allowed bin Laden and his operatives to remain free to plan in near total secrecy a devastating and coordinated series of attacks that would catch Americans—even intelligence officials—off guard and unprepared.

September 11

T he day dawned dazzlingly bright and sunny in New York City. The sky was a deep blue, and the air seemed remarkably clear, as if it has been washed clean by the torrential rainfall of the previous night. It was the kind of morning that inspired optimism and renewed energy, coming as it did after a long, hot summer. On this glorious September 11 morning, there was no indication that anything but changes for the better were in store.

America Under Attack

Soon after its takeoff from Logan Airport in Boston, American Airlines Flight 11 (bound for Los Angeles), with ninety-two people on board, was hijacked. At 8:46 AM, the plane crashed into the north tower of the World Trade Center. An estimated 20,000 people were in the building complex when the first plane hit. There could have been many more. Between 50,000 and 80,000 people worked in the World Trade Center each day.

Leonore McKean, a paralegal at Merrill Lynch at 222 Broadway, felt her building shake and looked out the window at the World Trade Center. "We saw people jumping from the high windows," she told the *New York Times*. Another witness said, "They looked like rag dolls being tossed."

3

Within just a few minutes, firefighters, police officers, emergency medical workers, and city officials were racing to the scene. Television screens across the country were tuned to live footage of the World Trade Center when United Airlines Flight 175 (from Boston, bound for Los Angeles), with sixty-five people on board, hit the south tower at 9:03 AM.

President George W. Bush was in Florida talking to young schoolchildren. An aide interrupted him and whispered something in his ear. About half an hour later, Bush made a short statement for the news cameras, saying that New York City had been attacked, but the United States would do everything in its power to hunt down the perpetrators. Yet the terror attacks were far from over.

At 9:40 AM, American Airlines Flight 77 (from Washington, D.C., bound for Los Angeles), with sixty-five people on board, crashed into the Pentagon, smashing through the walls of its southwest side and igniting a devastating fire, killing 190 people. At 9:45 AM, the Federal Aviation Administration (FAA) banned all aircraft takeoffs in the United States and ordered all planes in the air to land at the nearest available airport.

At 9:48 AM, the evacuations of the U.S. Capitol and the West Wing of the White House were begun. Vice President Dick Cheney was literally grabbed by the lapels by Secret Service agents and pushed out of his office and into an underground bunker. President Bush soon left Florida and spent much of the day flying on Air Force One in a zigzag path across the United States in an attempt to elude any would-be terrorists or assassins. It was now clear that the United States was under attack.

Hijacked United Airlines Flight 175 approaches the south tower of the World Trade Center seconds before impact. It was just eighteen minutes after American Airlines Flight 11 crashed into the north tower, which is shown belching smoke following the fuel-laden jet's crash and explosion. Shortly after its departure from Logan Airport in Boston, Flight 175 disappeared from radar screens and stopped responding to radio calls from air traffic controllers. The force of the plane's impact with the south tower and the damage that resulted caused the tower to collapse at 9:50 AM, only forty-seven minutes after it was hit.

At 9:50 AM, on a day already filled with unbelievable and horrifying occurrences, the unimaginable happened: The south tower of the World Trade Center suddenly collapsed into a densely packed pile of twisted metal. It sent a thick, billowing cloud of ash and dust throughout lower Manhattan. People watching the disaster on TV from all over the world knew that they were witnessing the deaths of thousands of people.

In lower Manhattan, a crowd had stood transfixed, staring up at the burning towers, watching in disbelief. As the debris cloud rushed toward them, they realized they had to get out of the area. Choking on the ash and dust that overtook them and turned midday into midnight, and cut by flying glass and chunks of rubble, they fled for their lives. Fire trucks and fleets of ambulances screamed past with wailing sirens, driving toward the remaining tower, as other rescue workers treated those who had just escaped.

At 9:58 AM, a 911 emergency operator in Pennsylvania received a call from a passenger using an air phone on United Airlines Flight 93 from Newark to San Francisco, with forty-five people on board. The plane was being hijacked, the passenger said. After reciting a prayer with the operator, the passenger, Todd Beamer, was heard to say to a group of passengers, "Let's roll!" Apparently, some passengers had organized a resistance effort against the hijackers. The voice recorder in the cockpit picked up the sounds of a fierce struggle with the terrorists. At 10:00 AM, Flight 93 crashed into a field eighty miles southeast of Pittsburgh, Pennsylvania. It was later theorized that the plane may have been headed for the Capitol or the White House in Washington, D.C. The passengers may have prevented a direct hit on the seat of the U.S. government and saved the lives of many government officials and workers.

People sprint up Broadway in lower Manhattan as a suffocating debris cloud from the collapse of the World Trade Center darkens the sky and races toward them. The rain of dust and ash was so thick that it turned a bright, clear, late summer day into darkest night in lower Manhattan, shattered windows, destroyed vehicles parked on the street, and left deep piles of ash and paper scattered over surrounding areas.

At 10:29 AM, the north tower of the World Trade Center collapsed, killing hundreds of trapped workers and rescuers who had rushed up the stairwells even after the first tower had fallen. Many other firefighters, police officers, and emergency medical technicians were killed as they assisted in evacuation and first-aid efforts at the base of the tower.

In New York, officials initially ordered 6,000 body bags, and later, in anticipation of even greater casualties, many more. In hospitals all over the city, thousands of New Yorkers lined up to give blood. New York City mayor Rudolph Giuliani ordered the evacuation of lower Manhattan to make it easier for 10,000 rescue workers to get to the scene.

Manhattan was in a state of "lockdown": All bridge and tunnel crossings were sealed, and its residents were stuck on what they suddenly remembered was an island. The U.S. Navy placed military forces in the Middle East and Europe on high alert. At a press conference, Mayor Giuliani, who had himself run for his life as the south tower collapsed while he was trying to set up an emergency on-site headquarters for rescue efforts, was asked how many people he thought might have died in the collapse of the World Trade Center. He replied that it was too soon even to think about that. As reported in the *New Yorker* magazine, he said only that it would be "more than any of us can bear, ultimately."

In the days that followed, New Yorkers watched as armored and machine-gun-mounted vehicles rumbled down the West Side Highway, armed National Guard troops stood at alert on street corners, Red Cross disaster relief vans sped down the city streets, and jet fighters circled in the sky. Heartbreaking images of those missing after the attacks were posted throughout New York City for many days following September 11, as thousands of people tried in vain to locate their friends and loved ones. These were the grim reminders of the new world that dawned on September 11.

America's Mayor

Major Rudolph Giuliani was a figure of controversy before the terrorist attacks on New York City, thanks mostly to his combative and opinionated style. Often sharp-tongued and impatient in his dealings with his political opponents, critics, and the press, he turned out to be the leader who knew best what to say and do in the aftermath of September 11. Almost single-handedly, he soothed and calmed a terrified and grieving city, and did so with grace, sensitivity, and extraordinary courage. Even New Yorkers who had disliked Giuliani for years began to feel a new affection for their mayor. To the entire country, he became a symbol of the city's resilient, unbroken spirit. A few months later, *Time* magazine put him on its cover as the Person of the Year—the individual who had done the most that year to influence world events. The magazine editors had hesitated a long time over this decision. The other choice would have been Osama bin Laden.

The Taliban Speak

Long before the day was over, world leaders across the political spectrum issued statements strongly condemning the attacks. Among them were the leaders of the Taliban, who ruled Afghanistan, sheltered Al Qaeda leader Osama bin Laden, and are now thought to have been intimately involved in and aware of the planning of the attacks. A Taliban spokesman added that Osama bin Laden could not be responsible. "Osama bin Laden cannot do this work, neither us. We are not supporting terrorism."

Rescue workers remove debris from the rubble of the World Trade Center on September 13, 2001. The search for survivors began minutes after the collapse of the second tower at 10:29 AM on September 11, but the work would drag on for many long and increasingly hopeless days. Two weeks later, the rescue mission was officially called off and shifted to a recovery operation. The search for bodies and the cleanup of the wreckage took eight months, officially ending on May 28, 2002. Almost two million tons of debris were hauled from the site during the operation.

In the days that followed, the United States began to learn the identities of the hijackers. The suspicion that Osama bin Laden's Al Qaeda network was responsible for the attacks grew stronger. The United States demanded that the Taliban hand Osama bin Laden over to the United States. The Taliban refused, saying he was their guest and, in any case, they did not know where he was. They claimed to have somehow "lost track" of him. The United States, taking this evasive and almost certainly deceitful answer as an implicit alliance between the Taliban and bin Laden, prepared for war in Afghanistan.

Ground Zero

Rescue workers came to New York from every part of the United States to help search for survivors in the rubble of the World Trade Center. Stunned New Yorkers, famous for their rough manners, expressed their gratitude with simplicity and openness, often volunteering to feed and comfort these rescue workers who were now experiencing their own trauma—the physical and psychological stress of laboring hour by hour, day upon day, in what amounted to a mass graveyard that yielded fewer survivors with each passing day. As the days wore on, the search for survivors shifted into an attempt to find bodies. This was no longer a rescue mission; it was now a recovery effort.

-The Investigation-

In October 2001, a U.S. bombing campaign was being waged in Afghanistan in response to the Taliban government's refusal to give up Osama bin Laden, who had quickly become the prime suspect in the September 11 attacks. With this American air support, an Afghan rebel group, the Northern Alliance, won the war against the Taliban and the Al Qaeda fighters the government had long supported and sheltered.

A Paper Trail

As Taliban and Al Qaeda members fled Afghanistan's cities in droves, U.S. soldiers and journalists moved in to gather the scraps of paper, file folders, notebooks, and computer disks left behind in order to gain whatever information they could about this once secret enemy. In two houses in Kabul, one belonging to the Taliban Ministry of Defense, documents were found describing Al Qaeda's interest in developing chemical, biological, and nuclear warfare capabilities. Apparently, despite having compiled a great amount of research—including old army manuals on explosives, scientific articles on poisons, diagrams of chemical agents, and studies on germ warfare vaccines—Al Qaeda was not able to acquire the necessary materials to produce any weapons of mass destruction. In addition to these documents, a flight simulator computer program and a list of U.S. flying schools were found in the abandoned Taliban

مُجاهد اِسلام
أسامه بن لادن

نُورِ خُدا هے کفرکی حرکت په خنده زن
پُهونکوں سے یہ چراغ بُجھایا نہ جائے گا

During a search-and-destroy mission in the Zhawar Kili area of Afghanistan, U.S. Navy SEALS (a special forces commando group that performs top-secret missions) found this Osama bin Laden propaganda poster in an Al Qaeda classroom on January 14, 2002. In addition to detaining several suspected Al Qaeda and Taliban members, the SEALs also found large caches of weapons and ammunition in numerous caves and abandoned buildings. To help eliminate the terrorists' infrastructure, the SEALs destroyed more than fifty caves and sixty buildings using ground explosives and air strikes.

offices. Some of the hijackers who flew the planes into the American targets on September 11 had enrolled in these same flight schools.

The "Twentieth Hijacker"

Some of the materials retrieved from abandoned Taliban and Al Qaeda offices and mountain hideouts documented plans for the attacks of September 11, 2001. Thousands of deaths could have been prevented if their contents had been known a few months earlier. Sadly, even without the discovery of these documents, law enforcement authorities did have an opportunity several weeks before September 11 to uncover and prevent the terrorist operation—an opportunity that was missed.

The owner of a flight school in Eagan, Minnesota, called the FBI and told them about a foreign student whose behavior was a bit peculiar. He wanted to be able to steer a jumbo jet but was not interested in learning how to land or take off. Could he be a potential hijacker? The flight school student, Zacarias Moussaoui, was arrested in August 2001 by the FBI on immigration charges. FBI field agents in Minneapolis asked the Justice Department in Washington for a warrant to search the hard drive on Moussaoui's computer. The request was denied because officials claimed there was not enough evidence to indicate that Moussaoui was a terrorist. This was despite the fact that an FBI agent in Arizona had also written a memo to headquarters expressing alarm at the number of Muslim students enrolling in flight schools in the United States. The FBI was suspicious enough to keep Moussaoui in custody, but they failed to launch a full investigation that might have uncovered the real conspiracy in time to prevent the September 11 hijackings and attacks.

Zacarias Moussaoui, a French citizen charged with conspiracy in the September 11 attacks on the United States, in an effort to avoid the death penalty, tried to plead guilty to some of the charges against him without admitting specific knowledge of the attacks. The judge pointed out that he could not plead guilty to conspiracy to commit acts of terrorism while continuing to claim that he was unaware of the hijackers' plans. Moussaoui withdrew his guilty plea and insisted he was not involved in the hijackings.

After September 11, law enforcement officials labeled Moussaoui the "twentieth hijacker" and concluded that he was a coconspirator. Like the other hijackers, he had received terrorist training at Al Qaeda camps in Afghanistan, had prepared for the attacks, and probably would have been on one of the hijacked planes if he had not been arrested on visa violations. At the time of this writing, he is charged with conspiring in the attacks and faces the death penalty.

A Different Kind of Suicide Bomber

Over the years, students of terrorism in the West have put together a profile of the typical suicide bomber. They picture a young man, eighteen to twenty-four years old, from a poor family, not well-educated, with all the outward signs of a religious fanatic. He would be the victim of a personal tragedy—such as a family member being killed by security forces or during a protest riot—that left him with nothing to lose. Becoming a martyr in a jihad would resolve all his personal problems, including financial difficulties. After his death, those who sent him on his mission would take better care of his family—using money raised for the terrorists' cause and earmarked for the "martyr's" survivors—than he would have been able to himself. The typical suicide bomber would be ignorant of the world of the "infidels" he planned to attack. This would help ensure that he would not develop any compassion for or sense of kinship with his victims, or become tempted by the Western lifestyle. The victims must never seem human to the suicide bomber but instead must be demonized.

This supposed suicide bomber mold was shattered, however, on September 11. The nineteen terrorists on the four hijacked planes that day were well-educated, experienced men, ranging in age from their late twenties to their mid-fifties. They knew their way around the West and had lived for several years in various Western countries. They obtained their flight training and made their final arrangements in the United States. They lived among Americans for months on end, in quiet suburban neighborhoods, but they apparently never wavered in their beliefs that

The Koran on Suicide

Many of Al Qaeda's attacks have been carried out by suicide bombers, men who knew that they would have to kill themselves in order to be able to kill others. Some terrorist leaders twist the teachings of Islam to their purposes as a way to inspire their followers to volunteer for these deadly missions. Would-be bombers are promised a painless death that bypasses the grave and a direct path to heaven. Yet most Muslim clerics point out that the Koran forbids suicide. It states that people who commit suicide will be punished in the afterlife by having to endlessly repeat the manner of their deaths. The Koran also lays down rules for warfare, forbidding the killing of women, children, and all civilians.

their neighbors were evil and inferior. Their desire to kill as many Americans as possible never diminished, even after being freely welcomed into the country and its schools and communities. Chillingly, they probably had a great deal of financial and logistical support from like-minded people living in the United States. It has been estimated that it took as many as 100 men to help the hijackers carry out the complex mission. They were "sleepers," living quiet lives of secret planning and preparation until the day the bloody deed was finally committed.

The FBI thinks that Mohamed Atta, a thirty-three-year-old Egyptian, was the commander of the operation. He was on Flight 11, the plane that included the highest number of hijackers who had had flight training. This plane crashed into the north tower

In this image from airport surveillance, two men, identified as suspected hijackers Mohamed Atta *(right)* and Abdulaziz Alomari *(center)*, pass through airport security at Portland International Jetport in Maine early on the morning of September 11, 2001. Authorities say the two men took a commuter flight from Portland to Boston, where they boarded American Airlines Flight 11, the plane they would hijack and crash into the north tower of the World Trade Center.

of the World Trade Center, the first strike of the day's series of assaults. Tracing Atta's movements after the fact, the FBI found that he had also looked into the possibility of buying a crop-dusting plane, perhaps hoping to use it to spread chemical or biological poisons over an American town, city, or water supply.

Flight School

In the months before September 11, 2001, Mohamed Atta and Marwan al-Shehhi practiced flying in small planes they rented at Huffman Aviation in Venice, Florida. Al-Shehhi was on board the plane that crashed into the south tower of the World Trade Center just minutes after the plane Atta was flying hit the north tower.

From July onward, their training intensified. They wanted to learn to fly the big passenger jets. For $1,500, they bought six hours of training time in a flight simulator at the SimCenter School in the town of Opa-Locka, Florida. The multimillion-dollar machine jerks and rocks like a ride in an amusement park. Airline pilots use it to train for emergencies too dangerous to practice in a real plane. Henry George, the owner at the SimCenter School, led Atta and al-Shehhi through the basic maneuvers. The simulator helped give them a sense of what it was like to handle an airliner.

Waleed Alshehri, a man in his mid-twenties who would be on Flight 11, was already a U.S.-trained pilot. In 1997, he had graduated from Embry-Riddle Aeronautical University in Daytona Beach, Florida. Another Flight 11 hijacker, Abdulaziz Alomari, took classes at FlightSafety Academy. He lived in Vero Beach, Florida, with his wife and three children, and told his landlord that he was a Saudi commercial pilot.

Hani Hanjour, thought to be at the controls of American Airlines Flight 77 when it flew into the Pentagon, had trained earlier at a CRM Airline Training Center in Scottsdale, Arizona. He was probably the best qualified pilot among the September 11 hijackers. By 1999, he had accumulated enough hours to earn a commercial pilot's license from the Federal Aviation

The CRM Airline Training Center in Scottsdale, Arizona. Hani Hanjour, one of the nineteen identified September 11 hijackers, received pilot instruction there in 1996 and 1997. Of the 19 suspects in the terrorist attacks, Hanjour had the deepest roots in the United States and seemed to have had the least contact with Islamic radicalism. *Inset:* Photos released by the FBI of the suspected hijackers aboard American Airlines Flight 77.

Administration. He lived most of the year before September 11 in a San Diego apartment complex with Nawaq Alhamzi and Khalid al-Midhar, two other men who were on board Flight 77.

Several of the hijackers were already on the FBI's list of suspected terrorists. For example, the Central Intelligence Agency (CIA) had information connecting Khalid al-Midhar and Nawaq Alhamzi to Al Qaeda. On August 23, learning that they might be in the United States, the CIA passed their names on to the FBI and the National Security Institute (NSI). The FBI searched the country but could not find the men's addresses until after September 11.

By then it was far too late. The secure world that we had once believed in had come to an end, changed beyond recognition, perhaps forever.

Conclusion

In response to the September 11 attacks, the United States officially declared a "war on terrorism." But what is that? Its objectives, strategies, and methods are difficult to determine because terrorism itself is so hard to define. One person's terrorist is another person's freedom fighter. After all, the rebellious American colonists were once considered terrorists by the English government.

Should violence committed against political and military targets by private individuals be considered terrorism, or is terrorism only violence committed against civilians? When the Nazis occupied France during World War II, the French Resistance blew up railroad stations and bridges and killed Nazi soldiers. By doing this, they violated a peace treaty that the French government had signed with Germany. To the Nazis and the collaborationist French government of that time, the Resistance was a terrorist group. Today, however, most people remember the Resistance as perhaps the noblest chapter in French history.

Though virtually all countries today say they are opposed to terrorism, many make exceptions for groups the United States defines as terrorists. For example, the government of Iran sees no contradiction in speaking out against terrorism while still supporting Palestinian Islamic Jihad and Hamas (Arabic for "zeal," or religious passion), groups that regularly send suicide bombers to blow up both soldiers and civilians in Israel. Iran regards Israel as an occupying force, and therefore sees Hamas as a resistance group.

A protester holds a portrait of Osama bin Laden during a rally against the United States on July 30, 1999, in Islamabad, Pakistan. While many in the international community see bin Laden as a criminal and a murderer, many Muslims view him as a sort of prophet, freedom fighter, and savior. His pro-Islamic religious rhetoric, violent anti-Western threats, shadowy and elusive presence, and rugged, wandering existence have inspired great loyalty and admiration in his followers. Many of them have demonstrated their willingness to die fighting for him.

It must be remembered that one cause of political violence around the world is the perceived lack of an alternative—some other means for powerless people to gain control of their future and to affect events. Where there is no wealth, no influence, no voice, violence may seem like the only way oppressed people

A participant in a massive rally in Lahore, Pakistan, organized by the country's largest religious/political party, Jamaat-I-Islami, holds a poster reading "Osama bin Laden is heartbeat of the Muslims." That sentiment is by no means a minority one among many Muslims throughout the world. While many of them may reject bin Laden's violent tactics, they still admire his defiantly pro-Islamic stance and his willingness to take on the largest Western military powers.

Conclusion

have to call attention to their plight and change things for the better. This is certainly true in the Middle East, and it is one reason why so many Muslims there admire Osama bin Laden. Without legitimate spokespeople and advocates, without representatives who have some persuasive influence over the leaders who make decisions and set policy, people start to see outlaws as heroes. A truly effective war on terrorism should nurture—not destroy—a climate in which the voices of the powerless can be heard.

Commentators like to remind us that the world is "more complicated" than it was before the September 11 attacks. This, of course, is inaccurate. The world was not any less complicated the day before September 11, 2001, than it was the day after. Ever since human communities began forming, the world has been a stage for complicated, violent, unjust, ugly, and occasionally beautiful and cooperative interaction. It is just that many of us in the West, lulled by a decade of prosperity and peace, thought we had the luxury of forgetting about trouble elsewhere in the world. Their problems were not our problems, we thought; their conflicts were not our conflicts. We know now that this was a mistaken assumption. After the Al Qaeda attacks of September 11, we again realize, for better and worse, just how involved we are in the world beyond our vulnerable shores.

Glossary

caliphate The reign of a successor to the prophet Muhammed's spiritual and secular leadership of Islam.

Central Intelligence Agency (CIA) A U.S. foreign intelligence organization that gathers and analyzes classified information and conducts secret operations outside the United States.

Cold War The more than forty-year ideological struggle between the United States and the Soviet Union, during which the two superpowers avoided direct conflict with each other because of the danger of nuclear war.

encryption software Computer programs that can be used to send secret, difficult-to-decode messages.

fatwa A religious decree based on the Koran.

Federal Aviation Administration (FFA) The U.S. agency that oversees airline safety.

Federal Bureau of Investigation (FBI) The U.S. agency charged with investigating interstate crimes.

flight simulator A machine that provides a convincing imitation of the experience of flying a plane.

Islam The religion of over a billion people on Earth, who follow the teachings of the Koran.

Islamic fundamentalism The political view that religion should dominate government in Islamic countries, with the law of the land based upon a strict and conservative interpretation of the Koran.

Glossary

jihad A holy war fought for Islam as a religious duty. Also, more generally defined as a personal struggle to follow a righteous path.

Marxists Followers of Karl Marx's theories about society and economics that included the equitable sharing of wealth and the destruction of restrictive class systems. The official belief system of the former Soviet Union.

mujahedeen (also spelled mujaheddin) Holy warriors on behalf of Islam.

National Security Agency (NSA) A U.S. intelligence organization that gathers secret information by high-tech means, such as through spy satellites and electronic decoding.

regime The group that holds power in a country.

relief worker A worker involved in a humanitarian mission, often employed by a nonprofit agency such as the Red Cross or the United Nations.

revolution A sudden, usually violent change in government that affects a whole society.

For More Information

Central Intelligence Agency (CIA)
Office of Public Affairs
Washington, DC 20505
(703) 482-0623
Web site: http://www.cia.gov

Council on American-Islamic Relations (CAIR)
453 New Jersey Avenue SE
Washington, DC 20003
(202) 488-8787
Web site: http://www.cair-net.org

Federal Bureau of Investigation (FBI)
935 Pennsylvania Avenue NW
Washington, DC 20535-0001
(202) 324-3000
Web site: http://www.fbi.gov

Federation of American Scientists (FAS)
Intelligence Resource Program
1717 K Street NW, Suite 209
Washington, DC 20036
(202) 454-4691
Web site: http://www.fas.org/irp/index.html

For More Information

National Security Agency (NSA)
Public Affairs Office
9800 Savage Road
Fort George G. Meade, MD 20755-6779
(301) 688-6524
Web site: http://www.nsa.gov

National Security Institute (NSI)
116 Main Street, Suite 200
Medway, MA 02053
(508) 533-9099
Web site: http://nsi.org

Terrorist Group Profiles
Dudley Knox Library
Naval Post Graduate School
411 Dyer Road
Monterey, CA 93943
Web site: http://library.nps.navy.mil/home/tgp/tgpmain.htm

Web Sites

Due to the changing nature of Internet links, the Rosen Publishing Group, Inc., has developed an online list of Web sites related to the subject of this book. This site is updated regularly. Please use this link to access the list:

http://www.rosenlinks.com/iwmito/alqa/

For Further Reading

Foster, Leila Merrell. *Afghanistan*. New York: Children's Press, 1996.

Foster, Leila Merrell. *The Story of the Persian Gulf War*. New York: Children's Press, 1991.

Fox, Mary Virginia. *Somalia*. New York: Children's Press, 1996.

Gordon, Matthew S. *Islam*. Rev. ed. New York: Facts on File, 2001.

Khan, Rukhsana. *Muslim Child: Understanding Islam Through Stories and Poems*. Toronto, ON: Napoleon Publishing, 1999.

Smith, Huston. *The Illustrated World's Religions: A Guide to Our Wisdom Traditions*. San Francisco, CA: Harper San Francisco, 1994.

Spencer, William. *Islamic Fundamentalism in the Modern World*. Brookfield, CT: Millbrook Press, 1995.

Spencer, William. *The United States and Iran*. Brookfield, CT: Twenty-First Century Books, 2000.

Stein, R. Conrad. *The Iran Hostage Crisis*. New York: Children's Press, 1994.

Wormser, Richard. *American Islam: Growing Up Muslim in America*. New York: Walker and Co., 1994.

Bibliography

Bergen, Peter. *Holy War, Inc.: Inside the Secret World of Osama bin Laden*. New York: The Free Press, 2001.

Beyer, Lisa. "The Most Wanted Man in the World." *Time*, September 16, 2001.

Bragg, Rick. "Streets of Huge Pakistan City Seethe with Hatred of U.S." *New York Times*, September 30, 2001.

Burke, Jason, Tim Judah, and Peter Beaumont. "Kabul Paper Trail Damns Al Qaeda." *The Observer* (London, England), November 18, 2001.

Connolly, Kate. " 'I Did What I Had to,' Says Suicide Pilot's Last Letter." *The Observer* (London, England), November 18, 2001.

Cronin, Anne. "A Black Cloud. A Shower of Glass. A Glimpse of Hell. Run!" *New York Times*, September 16, 2001.

Ellison, Michael, Ed Vulliamy, and Jane Martinson. "We Got Down to the Outside and It Was Like an Apocalypse." *The Guardian* (London, England), September 12, 2001.

Fineman, Mark. "Life Inside Al Qaeda: A Destructive Devotion." *Los Angeles Times*, September 24, 2001.

Girardet, Edward. "A Brush with Laden on the Jihad Front Line." *Christian Science Monitor*, August 31, 1998.

Laqueur, Walter. *The New Terrorism: Fanaticism and the Arms of Mass Destruction*. New York: Oxford University Press, 1999.

Lewis, Bernard. *Islam and the West*. New York: Oxford University Press, 1993.

Lewis, Bernard, ed. *A Middle East Mosaic: Fragments of Life, Letters, and History*. New York: Random House, 2000.

Longman, Jere. "The Pennsylvania Crash: Cockpit Tape Offers Few Answers but Points to Heroic Efforts." *New York Times*, March 27, 2002.

McGeary, Johanna, and David Van Biema. "The New Breed of Terrorist." *Time*, September 16, 2001.

Miller, Judith. "Osama bin Laden: Child of Privilege Who Champions Holy War." *New York Times*, September 14, 2001.

Olson-Raymer, Gale. *Terrorism: A Historical and Contemporary Perspective*. New York: American Heritage, 1996.

Risen, James, and David Johnston. "Tape Reveals Wild Struggle on Flight 93." *New York Times*, September 22, 2001.

"September 11." *New Yorker*, September 24, 2001.

Index

Index

terrorism, 4
   in East Africa, 24
   September 11, 2001, 4, 8, 9, 10, 19,
      24, 31–39, 40–49
   war on, 50
Time magazine, 19, 37

U

United Nations, 16, 18–19
United States,
   and Afghanistan, 11–12
   and Al Qaeda, 9
   and Iran, 22
   and Iraq, 16
   and Muslims, 9, 15
   secular lifestyle of, 9
   and Somolia, 18–19

W

Wahhabi, 10
Wall Street Journal, 27
"war on terrorism," 50
Washington, D.C., 4, 34
World Trade Center, 4, 24, 31–35, 39, 46

About the Author

Phillip Margulies is a freelance writer living and working in New York City.

Photo Credits

Cover, pp. 5, 6–7, 14, 26 (inset), 29, 33, 35, 38, 41, 43, 46 © TimePix; pp. 1, 17, 26, 48 © AP/World Wide Photos; pp. 11, 21, 51, 52 © Corbis.

Series Design and Layout

Nelson Sá

Editor

John Kemmerer